IT'S TIME TO EAT CHRISTMAS MELONS

It's Time to Eat CHRISTMAS MELONS

Walter the Educator

Silent King Books
A WhichHead Entertainment Imprint

Copyright © 2024 by Walter the Educator

All rights reserved. No part of this book may be reproduced in any manner whatsoever without written per- mission except in the case of brief quotations embodied in critical articles and reviews.

First Printing, 2024

Disclaimer

This book is a literary work; the story is not about specific persons, locations, situations, and/or circumstances unless mentioned in a historical context. Any resemblance to real persons, locations, situations, and/or circumstances is coincidental. This book is for entertainment and informational purposes only. The author and publisher offer this information without warranties expressed or implied. No matter the grounds, neither the author nor the publisher will be accountable for any losses, injuries, or other damages caused by the reader's use of this book. The use of this book acknowledges an understanding and acceptance of this disclaimer.

It's Time to Eat CHRISTMAS MELONS is a collectible early learning book by Walter the Educator suitable for all ages belonging to Walter the Educator's Time to Eat Book Series. Collect more books at WaltertheEducator.com

USE THE EXTRA SPACE TO TAKE NOTES AND DOCUMENT YOUR MEMORIES

CHRISTMAS MELONS

The snow is falling, the air is cool,

It's Time to Eat Christmas Melons

It's Christmas time, no need for school!

The table is set, the candles glow,

And Christmas melons steal the show.

Round and green, with stripes so bright,

They sparkle like stars on a winter night.

Inside they're golden, juicy, and sweet,

Oh, Christmas melons are such a treat!

"Come take a slice," says Mom with cheer,

The melon's magic is finally here.

Its scent fills the room, soft and light,

It feels like a hug on Christmas night.

The first big bite is a burst of fun,

Like sunshine under the frosty sun.

Drip, drip, drip, the juice runs free,

Christmas melon delight for you and me!

It's Time to Eat Christmas Melons

We share a slice with Grandpa Joe,

His smile is big, his cheeks aglow.

"Reminds me of summers long ago,"

He says with a laugh, his face all aglow.

"Melon for breakfast, melon for snacks,

Let's pack it up in holiday sacks!"

Says little Tim with a playful shout,

"Christmas melons are what it's about!"

We sprinkle on sugar or a pinch of spice,

Each way to eat it is equally nice.

A melon party, let's all dig in,

With every bite, the smiles begin!

By the fire, we pass it around,

The joy of Christmas in every sound.

Crunch and slurp, the room is alive,

It's Time to Eat
Christmas Melons

Christmas melon makes our spirits thrive!

When dinner is done, the plates are clear,

We save one slice for the reindeer.

A treat for Santa, so sweet and rare,

A Christmas melon shows we care.

So every year, we wait with glee,

For Christmas melons by the tree.

A holiday fruit so full of cheer,

It's Time to Eat
Christmas Melons

It's the sweetest part of the best time of year!

ABOUT THE CREATOR

Walter the Educator is one of the pseudonyms for Walter Anderson. Formally educated in Chemistry, Business, and Education, he is an educator, an author, a diverse entrepreneur, and he is the son of a disabled war veteran. "Walter the Educator" shares his time between educating and creating. He holds interests and owns several creative projects that entertain, enlighten, enhance, and educate, hoping to inspire and motivate you. Follow, find new works, and stay up to date with Walter the Educator™

at WaltertheEducator.com

www.ingramcontent.com/pod-product-compliance
Lightning Source LLC
LaVergne TN
LVHW010622070526
838199LV00063BA/5246